SURVIVING FRAGMENTS

Updated and Expanded

BOOKS BY MARC THOMAS

Surviving Fragments - 2024

Talking to the Machines

Listening to the Survivors:
Ghost Stories from the Recent Plague

Wetlands: Low Country Haiku

Poems of Resistance

SURVIVING FRAGMENTS

Updated and Expanded

MARC THOMAS

SAVANNAH, GA 2026

ISBN: 979-8-9925811-4-0

Cover Photo Credit: *The Curse of Artemisia -- Fragment*. [place of publication not identified: publisher not identified, 350 B.C. to 300 B.C] Image. Retrieved from the Library of Congress, <www.loc.gov/item/2021667677/>.

www.ruminatingpoetpress.com

For Margo

Contents

Prefatory Note
(Revised and Updated)

Herein, with little craft or discipline,
is an Assortment —
from Juvenilia
to Elder Crankiness,
with Occasional Epiphanies,
mostly old
but a few new additions,
slightly expanded
from the earlier edition.
No writing class
No workshop
No writers' group projects.
Here are bits and pieces
Accumulated
Moved from place to place
(some bits almost thirty times)
but
Not Revised for Consistency
and
finally
Typed, Cleaned Up, Reformatted,
Revisited and Reedited,
and
Presented for Your Entertainment.
Be thankful:
You remain ignorant
of the remnants
now discarded

as childish, foolish, confused,
or simply repulsive.
Having failed to track
when and where
these pieces
were written originally
(or derivatively, as it were)
and
Having long served as a Librarian,
the Surviving Fragments
are here presented
in
Alphabetical Order.

Ah, Lunch

When alone
Is made slowly,
Contentedly, with automatic motion
And no schedule.
Usually soup, bread,
with Milk or beer to
drink And poetry to
browse.

Today,
Chicken with mushrooms, *schmalzig*,
While visiting old Russia
And listening, half-attentive,
To twanging peasant music.

Sometimes,
I dip each bit of bread
And nibble it, cautiously, to keep
The drippings from my beard,
Off my book, while
Street fires scorch New York.

Right now,
Holding my book on my lap,
I break my bread
Into small squares
And drop them in.
I spoon
Soaked fatty gravy bread,
And think my body
Could never be somebody else's.

The milk is cold.
The bread is brown.
I drink and sip and read.

Alley on Garbage Day

Badly surfaced, unrepaired,
Cracked, stumbly
Feet slide on pebbles,
Twist, trip, slip
Nothing like the shopping mall
        polished
        floodlit
        planned and organized
        encouraging flow

Strolling slowly behind homes,
Sometimes chatting with the residents,
We survey the backs of houses,
Blocks of seemly fronts
These back roads of Baltimore
Reveal the hidden flaws
And beauty

(I didn't know a rose
        could be so orange)

Every day, it is amazing
What we throw away
Not just the rich
It's worth a look
Our home is full of happy finds
From trips like this today

A lot of people
Take the tour, you know,
So best start early
Some fellow scavengers specialize

magazines
appliances
worn-out tools
furniture
We wander and wait, until
Luck and fancy come together

The regulars
All nod to each other
And pass the word.
There are things to learn
And occasions to observe
spring-cleaning
new baby
moving out
moving on
deaths and evictions

These backyard bottles
Betray the prim front
There's just no telling
What people will eat

Here now, for me,
A novel sight
On trash day rounds

Stretched out,
Three feet from the cans,
Bikini in the sun,
Halter undone, dark glasses
And darkening grease

People pass by

And not a twitch
Of young firm breasts
Her suit pure white,
So small, so tight,
Face rested, lying loose
As passersby, the regulars,
Look her up and down
And then go check the next can

The truck drives on,
Clanking, groaning,
Starting, stopping,
Never quite seeming
To get a good start
The three-man team
Keeps the routine
        lifting
        throwing
        dumping
        cans and boxes
        leaves and branches
        plastic bags
        and a little chatter
All into the churning maw
As she lies unmoving,
They round her corner,
Noisy, smelly, obtrusive

Bang, and the can is lifted,
Emptied, put down again
Bang, strong hands seize her
        clamp her mouth
        strip her
        pass her up the truck

stuff her in the cab
fill her, empty her
set her down again

Laughing, they throw her glasses,
Her scrap of suit, to where she sits
The truck drives on,
Clanking, groaning

The pickers, as we call ourselves,
Glance back passively,
Then move on
Ahead of the truck,
Clearing the way

We made out pretty well today
    a window box
    a lamp base
    a current catalog
    assorted glimpses and memories
Not remarkable, perhaps,
But satisfying

Let's go on home,
and have another cup of coffee

A Small Transcendence

I worshiped reason,
Proclaimed lucidity
Both sacred and profane.
Wielding words like cold knives
Excising my old friends'
Most cherished impossibilities.

So control, raised to unfeeling,
Mistaken for "objectivity,"
Was my pretense at expressing myself.
I became, practiced, a skilled player,
Both tongue and mind
Registered with the police.

Hypocrisy might have saved me,
But my great pride and small self-
knowledge
Prevented me.

Small errata of my actions,
My unintended insults, petty errors,
Lost desiderata,
Accumulated like dust in a machine.
This love, fear of dentists,
The book unread but cherished,
Inertia, and the pleasure of a day,
The friend enjoyed without reproach,
Have worn down vanity.

Disillusioned, I am less satisfied,
But am more free and able to use
The tool I once abused.

Books

Lives on my shelves, stacked-away days.
Gravel raked, rocks all in place.
Flowers gathered in bright bunches.
Something to suit every motion
Of my friendly face, or to creep
Into the crevasses of my secret selves.
Counters in my many games, picked pieces
Placed up front to daunt the enemy,
Reserves held back for rescue or surprise,
Trumps played out with timely finesse.
Never able to fix you in my selfish sky,
Or name you into constellations, still,
You are more the measure of myself
Than astrology or the painted cards.
No height or place limits you, or me.
You settle always in delightful pattern,
New light and color reveal you,
By both chance and manipulation.
An ever-changing kaleidoscope
Of new combinations and relations.
Oh, you grow, you pile up,
You spread out and up,
Large and heavy in all my house and life.
Yet I welcome you and am not overwhelmed,
But for a moment. Though at times tired,
Wading slow-legged through your swamps,
Climbing too high with unneeded baggage.
Still, when all complaint and guilt
Are put aside, and honesty prevails,
I must say of you, my books,
You've opened me, as I have opened you.

Cat

slanted eyes, slitted eyes,
narrow muzzle, whiskers,
construct an alien countenance.
alert ears, coiled tail,
legs tightened and ready,
suggest a tense serenity.

why does this face,
always without expression,
seem an exotic woman?

how does this beast,
without voice or song,
convey a strange intelligence?

doubtless it does not,
only takes things as they come,
not knowing the fancies it arouses
in a man's mind imagining
          another animal like itself.

The Catch

is in the throat
and down
under the
sternum.
The skin on the temples

tightens, strains, sweats,

but
is only felt,
not
seen.
A fine film of fear
coats the
body —

odors rise
from forehead, arms,
chest,
back, belly,
knees
and
— drips,
drips down
the back,
between the
cheeks of the ass.

The
eyes

open wider

dilate.

Hands
clench clammy palms,

and thumbs
number fingers.

Nostrils
spread and scoop,

sucking deep, as
the chest,
muscles and
ribs,

opens
like a
bellows
and a new rush of air
slides
down the throat
and releases the Catch.

Caught

we are all caught
in a web of blood
a tangle of births
groping connections
crises cross the world
bridge boundaries and prejudices
and yet are powerless
to push back hatred.
the camouflage of love
too often hides distaste
we track clumsily
through sticky deposits
left by passing genitals
gripping in great desperation.
an intersection unadmitted
by all but the most open.
a few stand aloof
spurning or spurned
repulsed by the fleshly contact
or hypnotized by the snake
but in some afterlife
they may in horror find
that souls too have their ways
of squirting and dripping
leaving a honey trail
across Elysian fields.

Coffee

Acutely
Alert and anxious
Every option offers
Uncountable consequences.

The mind
        darts
and flits   about
Around, round, and through.
        Unsettling.
(and the digestion)

Hands flutter,
        the eye
Can not set.   If
I were not aware
Of my own internal states
Then who?
        would take care.

It is resolved then.
In pursuit of serenity,
Never again three cups.

Complaints

As a child they never tell you
Of the small pains
Perhaps they did not notice
Or ever stopped to count

Commercials know
Of migraine, sinus, heartburn
Constipation, or its opposite,
Stiffened joints, dry or runny eyes,
Are our common inheritances

It hurts every day
But it's not important

We all kvetch
A little (or much)
Complain and gripe
Or whine as we unwind
A way of life
A kind of conversation
And a form of entertainment

Currents

Bodily fluids
Carry and drive us
A drama of pure
Hydrodynamics
Sex and violence
(adulterated crude modern reductions
        of revered love and death)
Could be writ as formulae
Of the flow of blood and jism
        Our most minor movements
        Seem subject to tides
        Amniotic, phlegm, and pus
        Salvation in salivation
        Go with the flow
        But any enumeration
        Of these lively liquids
        Will never afford
        advice Just description
        Neither elevated nor debased
                How describe a river
                From sitting on a bank?
                We can count, collect, and categorize
                The flotsam carried down the flood
                We can estimate its age
                And search for ancient beds
                Or yet gather the debris
                From banks, basins, and backwaters
                And hopefully deduce
                What did go down
                And what did not
                        Or cast lines, nets, and spears
                        To sample what's concealed

Beneath the flashing surface
Carefully collate our samples
Stored in bottles, jugs, and vials
And yet we can assume
That something will escape
But never will we learn
The seductive secrets of the river

So is history, so is man
Our heroes and great leaders
And our fathomless fantasies
Flotsam on the flood of common
    blood
While the mass remains a
    mystery

Dark Man

Moving slowly, visor closed
The dark helm encasing his head
He stubs and pokes with a wary stick
Testing height, texture, solidity
Of obstacles at long distance

Feeling forward with his long white fingertip
The world is known
As one moving point
Introjecting an unlit scene
Into the bone tube

A thousand sounds surround him
Falling like blown leaves on his open skin
Heat climbs and fills his trembling nose
Which, unwarned, must accept it all

Abstractions are the forms we know best
As silhouettes and screens
Our flat and simple reductions,
But for him, no thing exists
Unless extended three ways
With form coming first to mind
          As a cupped hand

Dell — 1978

I.

Down in the city
Down, within, below
Recessed
Insulated
A cool island dell
Surrounded
By wooded slopes
Stone walls
Invisible streets
And above the trees
Baltimore
And peaks of buildings
Down here,
Distant traffic rumbles
A pale white noise
Above which birds call
Lovers and musicians,
Cyclists, sunbathers, and softball,
Frisbees, family cookouts,
Strollers, children and alcoholics
Justify, preserve
This elegant lacuna
In the urban mass

II.

Ah, sunbathers
What a pair
Exhibitionist strut
Two-piece dance band
Rhythm section
Carrying towels and beer
Hipflicking walk

Out to dead center
Hogging the stage
With poses of indifference
Take off
Shirts and shorts
Spread the towels
Turn on
The tunes
Roll the suits
As small as possible
Stretch and oil

III.

Down come the drunks
Commandeering the conveniences
Long benches
Breezy shade
Trash cans
Seclusion
Public restrooms
They descend
To sleep in the sun
Swap lies and brown bags
And stay away
From censorious eyes
To come down
Down here

IV.

Another pair
Long and lean
Brown, blonde, and bony
Both beauty and the baitFor
her friend, White-skinned
Short and wide Slackbellied

Tightsuited
Hips and breasts rolling over
Small and inadequate elastic
Hungry, but shy

V.

In season, the mating game
Of lovers of their own sex
Old and young
Affectionate or
Mercenary
Fill the park
With shrill clack
Of anxious bitchiness
Some conflicts arise
Between the out and open
And the more discrete,
A disturbance
In signs and nuance
Some seem suspicious
More of each other
Than their tolerant public
But still,
Down here is peaceful
Truce established
Mixed couples sprawl
Around the large trees
And the unmixed sun
Near the monument

VI.

Accessories and anatomy
Carefully arrayed
Their scene is set
Now the play begins
Pop-tops
Bottoms up
Fill and light
A passing ipe
Change stations
The sounds and scents
Ebb upon the air
Guys pass by, turn
And pass again,
Ask for a match
Offer a cigarette
With perfect nonchalance

VII.

There is a playground
Up near the corner
Near the monument
Where the longest benches
Are the best seats
For watching passersby
Old men
May be irritated by the children
But tolerate them
So they, the old men,
Can watch the young mothers

VIII.

Pale skin
Whitebelly

Tries to shake it
loose Turns the
music louder
Starts to dance
But the passing fancies
Are still attached
To long brown bones
So she gives it up and
Stretches in the sun again
Most men merely linger
But a moment, then go on,
Though eventually two
Stop and stay awhile
T-shirts, tattoos, and
Motorcycle helmets
Their bikes must be
Invisible

IX.

The kids
Rush all over
Only a few ever stay
Up by the playground
There are paths
Through the heavy brush
They hoot happily
As they pretend to hide
We may be afraid
Of what they find
But there is no way
To protect them

X.

Taut and tanned
Continues the conversation

The quiet one
Stretches and
rearranges Her wobbly
flesh, Crawling on all
fours Around the radio
Hoping to hide her belly
And reveal her breasts
This afternoon
Must be considered a success
It stretches indefinitely
A foursome now

XI.

The damned dogs
Are always around
They are either
Brought or they
come
Though we don't like them
We prefer them to their owners
The dogs are better bred
They are helpful
With balls and frisbees
And keep us on alert
So far we've been lucky
None of us
Has slipped in shit
The natures of dogs and men
Unpleasantly unfold
Through the problem
Of obedience
Down Boy,
Down

XII.

Oh, pale and mousy,
Hungry, unspeaking,
Do your show
Limbering exercises
Pulling up, rolling tight
Your bikini bottom
Too bad you can't roll up
Your reddening flesh
Let your straps fall
Give your whole body
To the hopeful rays
Stand and stretch now
Dance and smoke
Crawl again on all fours
And drink on, giggling

XIII.

The lawns are green
Trees and walls a shelter
The breezes constant comfort
Even down here some
Bad things go down
Under the serenity
The roots of this island
Are cloyed with turds
With broken glass
With pop-tops and bottle caps
Some people bring
Here their troubles, and some
Leave them behind

DINER

the old neon sign
still says
OPEN 24 HOURS
but its lights
are dark

below,
a sign on wheels
announces
NEW HOURS
NEW MENU
BEER AND WINE
and that is probably true

but
it won't replace
the memories
of burnt coffee
free refills
and cold pie
at a gritty 3 AM

Distant Relation

The talk here
Is always filled with silence

I am afraid

of all things left unsaid

Someday,

I will stand and speak
without uncertainty

If

they promise before I speak

not to listen

Dog Tales

Nothing is better
After a long walk
Than to carry a good stick home.

Let me run!
I'll come back!
As soon as I lose the scent
Or it goes cold.
Or, if nothing else,
I get tired and miss you.

O, wad some power the doggie gie us
To smell ourselves as others see us.
It wad frae monie a vanitie free us
To know we all sweat and pee.

Stand in your yard and Bark!
I am here! My yard! I am here!
And how good to hear
Answer from neighboring yards
Me too! I am here! My yard!

It's nice to be led on a walk,
But,
Why won't the damn walker
Let me finish smelling?

It snowed!
And I ran, and ran, and snorted,
And got wet and cold
And you dried me and let me on the couch.

Running flat out,
Running tongue out,
Running nose down,
Baying scents loud,
Is perfect!

Nose to tail, circled,
Curled in the sun and leaves,
Then — instantly — BARK!

Shake, shake, shake shake, shake!
If I keep shaking, I can
Kill this squeaky toy!

There is nothing I can say
        about my doggies
That the wagging flags of their tails
        do not tell better.
True dogs have no names.
Their bodies are the signifiers
        Scent
        Tail
        Posture
Voices belling, barking, whining
Emanating identity.

Dogpile

Young boys yell
"DOGPILE"
Announcing opportunities
        for malice
        bullying
        revenge
In the midst of play

In the primal pile
There may be
        pushing for position
        even, rarely, a nip
Dogs know it is for all
        comfort
        warmth
        belonging
At the end of day

Evening Event: After-Dinner Mysticism

Lightning —
        a vivid red roof

Crack of following sound
        then the slush of traffic
        tap, on the roof tar, tapping

Bound to my senses
        lashed to the mast of my body

In search of visions
        the line of black worms
        crawling through consciousness
        I follow them, page by page,
        hoping for holy books

When I raise my eyes
        Here I am again
        Nothing possesses me —
        the fancies, strong words
        remain but in memory

I am held fast by
        weather outside my window
        coffee, couch, paper, pen
        constant questions from my boys

All my beloved anchors

Fancy Apes

I. Introducing the Animal

Here we go again
Thinking that walking upright
Opposing our thumbs
Posing our big heads and long limbs
Standing erect above it all
Talking, and talking, and
Reasoning all our reasons
Removes us from the raw truths
        the hairy body
        the ancestral fears
        the bloody birth
        the infant suck
        the sweats and hungers
        the daily busyness of feeding our
                hungry selves
        the lusting humpings, matings
        the flight, fight, or freeze
        the chest thumping, and cowering
        the push for dominance
                the rage of challenge
                the humiliation of loss
        the clumping together
                for comfort
                and grooming
                to chatter and share
                to huddle in fear
                to share food
        the alliances and deceptions
O wise and noble animal
        we are deluded

II. The Fancy Apes Start a Meeting

Basic fieldwork practice
In observing fancy apes
In their natural habitat
Is to get there early
And fade into the background

The Monday morning staff brief
is a good place to start
Arrive by 8:45
And find the darkest corner

First the Chief Assistant
Will straighten out the Chairs,
Wipe down the Table,
Check the video and mic,
then sit behind the Big Head's seat and wait

Next come the Little Heads,
some with their own Aides
(whose distinguishing marks are inferior tailoring
and obsequiousness,
except for the very pretty ones),
who claim seats around the Table
based on hope, presumption,
or perhaps unvoiced anxieties.

The spots nearby the Big Head's seat
often are the last to fill,
but anomalies can occur
if one or more of the Little Heads
plans a major move,
or postures as Contender,

or is to be the scapegoat

Big Head, of course,
comes last,
is First but always late,
still talking on the phone,
assessing, checks the attendees and positions,
sits upon the Throne,
and Starts the Meeting

III. Mating Habits

It is harder to observe
Mating Habits in the Field
in these smartphone days of dating sites, social
media, apps, and other electronic substitutes
for physical sociality

The better places to set up your Blind
(still) are
barrooms and events
Or the primal watering hole,
unmarred by modern media,
such as the Church Social

The Observer may exploit
a Traditional and Structured Event
to acquire
Advance Intelligence,
which enables
Systematic Observational Categorization

The Observation Plan

should include
a Categorization Taxonomy,
defining the X and Y Axes.
Examples of Critical Variables may include:
Single, Attached, Newly Resingled
or
Member, Stranger, Cousin.
(Previous studies deployed
Three Dimensions,
but data now show that
Gender may be ignored)

The Observer should note for each
Observed Interaction
which Party
Approaches, Introduces, Smiles.
Which of the Observed
Cluster among the Familiar,
and which Venture among the Strangers.
Note especially, when Bringing in the Strangers,
Incidents of Brazen Posturing,
Glances, both furtive and direct,
and, especially,
Touching, Laughing
and
Hiding in Corners

If possible,
the Observer
Should install game cameras
At the Drinks Table, and
in the Kitchen

IV. Ten Thousand Things

The pivotal difference
between the Fancy Apes
and common ones
is creation and proliferation
of the Ten Thousand Things

Common Apes
make do with little,
Perhaps some sticks and stones
to aid in eating
Or a nest of leaves and branches

Fancy Apes
prize possessions
and have created
not just Things
but Thing Makers
Thing Storers
Thing Fixers
and Thing Breakers,
Apparently with the Goal
That each member of the Species
Has their own Ten Thousand Things

The Observer
must take care
not to jeopardize the Things,
else the Observed
will target the Observer
with all Deception
and Force
at their command

V. Moving Together in Time

Almost all Apes assemble,
but the Fancy Apes
have forged
new forms of gathering,
in which the
Proud and Old
employ a ritual primacy
not observed with other Apes

It all began
with fireside tales,
but has evolved in
myriad forms,
from
song and dance
to massive groups

First,
the Hunt and Harvest,
followed by the Feast of Sharing.
Later, with farms and towns, the Building,
of a Barn, or a Palisade.
Later yet, for The Warrior Band,
a Hall

Art and Power combine
in Parades and Concerts,
Power and Force combine
in Police and Armies,
Rage and Confusion combine

in the Mob

The Observer
must be careful,
and to survive
must join or run

VI. The Old Ape Considers

Long ago having
Been assigned to
Watch the Watchers,
We must consider
What They and We have come to

We are documented
Measured
Counted
Recorded
Filmed
Observed
Classified
Categorized
Nominated and Denominated
Investigated
Fumigated
Ruminated
and
Fed a Load of Hogwash

And yet Observers
have failed to report
that

They, like We,
all age and die

All We can do
is strike a
balance
of
Struggling
Enduring
Rejoicing
Loving
and Getting On
As best we Can

Fat

Of course I understand –
We need only to right
The ratio of meals to exercise.
Yet this simple formula won't suffice to shift
My inertia into action,
As implied.
Of course I understand –
Though I doubt that I'll give up
This comfort through a little act of will.
My life is settled now,
My flesh with it, y'know,
And it's always so much easier to sit still.
I need a flash of heat, or some rush of energy,
To start the change from wish to happy act.
The accumulated wastes stripped from this
fleshy frame
Would unveil a purer self. That is a fact.
It sounds like giving up, to stodgily resist
In face of all the arguments for loss.
But that future self's a hope; while the old one
still is here,
Unconvinced that it must sacrifice its dross.
Though the healthy will deride, and the lovely
will be snide,
My decision's to remain a tub of lard.
My life is settled down, with its flesh spread all
around,
And to change this part for that is just too
hard.

Garrote

slow, melancholic, tired and restless
        dim ambition stirs the gut
        a sigh whistles in the throat
if he could just be cured of itches
        he could create

but fleas infest his clothes
        and the black rings of his fingernails
        distract

it would be easier to think, to be
        inspired
        if the tooth did not ache
        if the tongue would forget
to explore the cold sore
        blooming under the lower lip

a million mystics must have lost their visions
        cast down
        by flatulence, fear, and flies

how the mind could soar
                                        if
it did not have to bear
        this burdened body with it

God Less

Who should play God?
It is so hard
To be serious about this question
How can we not play God?
Short of miracles, or shared visions,
There is no one else around

It is the Great Good God
Who causes all the problems
An Athenian would not give pause,
Knowing gods capricious,
And that to play a god
Was only to pretend to power

We make our choices fearfully,
Culpable of ignorance,
Weakly incapable of great good,
Clearly capable of great evil
We make the safe choice
And pretend to small virtues
By refusing responsibility

Haiku

The doe and her fawn
Stop and stand in the clearing,
Look! And bound away

#

Young alligator
Basking on the grassy shore,
Rises, slides to the hunt

#

Two young green herons,
Barely able to fly well,
Clown across the sky

#

Seeing the full moon
Through the gap between branches
I lose track of time

#

Marshland at high tide
Grass and water intermingling
Exchanging edges

Two fawns, fox squirrel,
Great and little blue herons,
An alligator

#

Perched on a dark stump,
Scummy water surrounding
A single wood duck

#

O! A rainbow cloud!
High cumulus ice crystals
Burst into color!

#

The amber river
Flows to a sandy puddle
Such a happy dog!

How It Is

Here you are, in your body
Body is first, before word or thought or dream

You are animal, mammal, human
A warm-blooded being that bears live young
Eating, drinking, pissing, shitting
Fluids of life, intake, output, breath, snot, vomit, phlegm
Sweat, pus, semen, egg
Blood, bile, lymph
Sexed — you breed — your body spreads
Tissues and organs are you but not you

System within system
What is a cell, what makes it work
Proteins, enzymes, neurotransmitters
Leukocyte, erythrocyte, ganglia, bones
Liver, heart, brain, gut, spleen, lungs
Parasites, symbiotes, hidden hangers-on that sometimes help or hurt

Complex, continuous, incomprehensible

In and out, all around,
never still, never thinking
You are birthed, you are fed, change and grow, age and die
It feels like more than that

You are
alive
breathing

reading
in a room, or out
on the earth
the skies above, the ground below
made of atoms
made of particles
located in space, in time,
in spacetime, if you can conceive it
still the moon hangs, spinning about the earth
spinning around the sun
spinning through the galaxy
spinning in this universe
beginnings theorized but unknown
ends certain, but far away
engulfed in
    dark energy,
    dark matter,
    dark knowledge,
    dark unknowns,
    unknowable unknowns

Intrusion in a Formal Garden

Stones
Cut and dressed
Laid in rough squares
Fine sand linking them
Turf
Cut and rolled
Laid in long lines
Fine grass close-groomed
Fountain splashing, pool lapping

Sun and breeze in April
Neck and scalp in warm noonlight
But the moist air is chilly
Forehead cool, placid thought
There is a sense of distance

This fervid work at order
Poses problems
The sand bright between the stones
The new-set turf intrusive
The benches spaced
With false and casual indifference
Rugged forms give awkward witness
They are handsome but unwelcoming

Yet beauty lives here
In the sound of water
In the fountain's patina
In the murk of the rain-roiled pool

Knowledge

comes slow and crooked
crippled by true and false
killed by right and wrong

knowledge
may creep or leap
is always
the most recent correction

knowledge
pays its way
copies, but does not borrow
saves, but also spends
and does not hoard

knowledge
moves like seed
hides like light
grows from death

wisdom
is the descendant
of a thousand stillbirths

Laundromat: Fragmentation

Dreary, unrewarding chores
release the spirit.
Whirring, warm scents,
a polite ignorance,
Combine to force detachment.
Ritual of duty
Purified in dinginess
Vulnerable anonymity.
Next to me,
Machine whines and thumps,
threatening to explode.
My testicles creep up,
and stomach tightens,
As imaginary shards
Spin out
Rip through
As I lay dying
Dripping in the damp clean clothes.
Somehow,
This moist and odorous atmosphere
Begets idiots,
Who mill and honk happily among
themselves.
I wonder if
Generations of public washing
Has spawned mutations
Wandering gaits
Lumpish tongues
Squat distortions.
The filthy Norse grew long and straight
compared to these.
Speed Queen Venus, with her Coke machine,

rising from the suds.
Except for your tiny waist
and your tight jeans
You would be unremarkable.
Your gum smacks and sticks
on your bad teeth.
Not pretty, or even symmetrical,
just poor and hard,
You provoke without hope of satisfaction
for yourself or others.
But your waist, a handspan small, gives
Shape to your ass
Thrust to your small breasts
Strut to your awkward walk.

It thrums and hums.
Smoke rises, heavy in the steamy air,
From drooping waiting fingers.
Chlorine bites the nose.
A clean strong square
brown woman
Folds, and folds, and folds
Clothes in
bright piles.
Humming in the hum,
I step outside
To stretch, and look around, and get away.
Among the trucks and sirens
Baltimore bells and hooves
approach and stop,
The Araber hollers
"STRAWBERRRRIES"
Declining to buy, retreating, returning,
humming again,

I move my load from box to box
                and sit and wait some more
Whining voices rise
                and itemize
The wrongs of unknown neighbors
                and I guess
This anonymity equates to privacy
                for some people.
Young girls pass in and out
                awash in giggles and secrets,
Flirting with windows and cars, perhaps
                just for practice.
Compared to the commercials,
                we are all indifferent.
Without brighter lights,
                or even a fresh scent,
We stack the gray and yellow
                with the worn.
Perhaps competitive cleanliness
                was just a fad.
Drying, I ponder the place of poetry
In worlds of politics, wealth, and woe
                and dirty clothes.
Things which send me in a spin.
                Can writing, or reading, ever
really represent life?
Unless anchored by a page
                my thought flies.
(I mix my whites and colors.)

Disputes about the pros and cons of preferred machines
                expose the halfwits,
And benches furnished for convenience

not comfort
Are littered with campaign rubbish, as if
This city could one day produce
a clean machine.
Intuitively, I am an anarchist, and use
whatever detergent is on sale
that day.
Rationally, ethically, I am a
socialist,
although I often dream,
materialistically,
of owning my own
washer and dryer,
as I am often antisocial.
Other times I
tend to think
that changing any thing
May bear a greater risk
than letting it change itself,
Though I would not let my children
always choose their own clothes.

If we were to take the family,
or the laundromat,
As my model of society,
either one a thing of dread,
I could find
no retreat
from rule by elite.
Hopes and fears mingle and jingle
and spin with the socks.
By chance I may get
a matched pair.

Somebody's unbalanced load
Thumps and rattles.
It threatens
Universal destruction,
But though we hear
We do not listen,
Just nod and say,
"Now, now, you're almost done."
Against all odds,
We're right again.
My sour coffee's done,
As is my load.
I pat it, and pack it, and stack it just so.
Then grunting and puffing, back home I go.

Letter Replying to a Friend

It has been a long time,
So it will be again.
Although we all have suffered,
Some of us have grown;
We remain much the same.
I keep many hopes
Which you cannot fulfill.
We are, again, beginning anew.
Although we are all damaged,
No one here is broken or dead.
Remember,
We have been known to laugh.
We steer well clear of buoys
That mark despair and defeat
Except when we are left adrift.
Do you fare any better?
Have you ever been entered by ecstasy?

Loss

There are odd blessings in loss
Flood, fire, or just a move
Can strip you
Suddenly, or bit by bit,
Of all the small material things
Which you have used to fill
Empty compartments of your life

The pang, true pain,
Discovering the loss
(Or the choice of it)
Can bring the first appreciation
That these little bits have known
From you, or anyone,
Since stored away

This hurt, bright and strong,
Is a better end
To the illusion of ownership
Than to have all the unexamined
Storerooms of the days of your life
Become valueless
On the day of your death

Meditating in a Kitchen

If we ever recover alchemy
It will be by cooking

Only an incantation or
Act of demonic will
Can save these fey concoctions
(and our fickle digestions)
From making some mortal mutation

Watch the hot mists rise
From roiling, oiled waters
Scent the ancient herbs
And dust of dried dead plants
Writhe about in steam
Settle on exposed skins
Coiling liquidly down
Down into depths of lungs

Mystic measure, immeasurably applied
Uncertain heat, inaccurately controlled
By inner elf of whim and fancy
Or necessities of substitutions,
All contribute to the chancy cauldron

There must be magic here,
for We not only decline to die
But it is seldom that we fail
To eat well as well as find delight

Monday Visit to the Medical School

It's been a life-and-death day
Some Mondays are like that
Other days too, but Mondays do it best
The sky was in mourning, gray as a dove
Damp air cloyed my skin
Like the chill from a stone crypt wall
I walked my child around the old dead cat
Cowardly quietly, unwanted questions in wait
Pleased when he did not notice

All day my breathing startled me
As if it did not belong
Behind the old red bricks
   People hurried
To repair the broken
And prepare the empty bodies
Inattentive to the noble portraits
Hung above and all around

Later, I watched the sun
Open bright and sudden
Across white-markered hills
With the drying of the damp
Life and death arose as odors
Pungent and inseparable

My Living Will

I love to be with you
to talk
to play and argue
to walk
to work together
to view this world through your eyes
to touch and to hold hands
When I cannot, when I no longer know you,
I am gone already, let me go

To be is to be with nature
the birds
the changing light
the wind in the trees
the shifting colors of water
the glimpse of fawn
the red fox
the circling hawk
the huge scoop of migrating pelicans
the crash and charge of storm
the sounds of the dawn chorus
fading though it is
When I cannot see or hear them
I am gone already, let me go

I love reading; even more, I love books
lost in a novel
puzzled by arguments
found in debate
caught in history's churn
moved or stilled by poetry
wondering and reasoning

piling book upon book
    tracing references
    deciphering obscure passages
    and wandering through
    the familiar and comforting hush
    of the library stacks
the little thrill of a new treasure
    the book in the mail
    the thrift store catch
    the surprise in the roadside library
    the gift of a friend
And when I cannot read or open or hold these books
I am gone already, let me go

Natural, Organic, Whole

It has been a problem to decide
what is and what is not.
I've often wondered
how things come to be
Which are nothing or never or not.

If we be purists,
Must we build
A pyre of hybrid crops?
Let us forfeit all control
And concede to circumstance.

How like a cell all things are.
Primeval primary processes
support us still, even at this
excessive evolutionary elevation.

To rise above, to see the whole,
we must see ourselves
not as pinnacle but particle.

These Institutions
These cities, nations, universities,
Camouflaged in monuments,
bricks and papers,
Are animals,
And we their bones and blood,
Our words and songs their skins.

We are not in the path of the storm,
We are the wind.
Our gusts blow with and against all others.

All life is dust, tossed in fluids,
    Suspended, dissolving, settling.

A lens will focus, or even diffuse,
    all light that passes through.
    So words may enlighten or blind the world
    As staring into the sun, even at eclipse,
        can destroy your vision.

The bad things come not from essence,
    but from lack or excess.
The good not from purity,
    but from balance.
We must not avoid difficult distinctions.
    Fine points require sharp minds,
        And measured scales.

On the Insufficiency of Language

I lie in bed early in the morning
The digital clock says [4:00]
I struggle to orient myself within
the space-time continuum
on the North American continent
tectonic plates drifting slowly
as the earth spins, rotating on its axis,
careening in its orbit
Gaia dancing with Luna
around the Sun, which, in turn, is
burning and spinning and moving
through its arm of our home galaxy
and the galaxy itself,
spreading among others
away through, expanding
and accelerating, since,
perhaps, the Big Bang
the evolution of life
its origin in the muck and pools of
shores and tides and borderlands
its first simple cells
then the hybrid eukaryotes
its symbionts and parasites
its plants and animals
its sun eaters, earth eaters
its herbivores, carnivores, omnivores
all devouring each other and thriving
on transformations of sunlight
the rise of this fancy ape that we call,
variously, Man and Us and Them
small bands that travel from ancestral
homes

tamers of fire, makers of tools
endlessly restless, gather and hunt
farm and fight and irrigate and trade
build castles, towns, and markets
cross seas, erect great walls
that enclose and divide and conquer
makers of kings and kingdoms and
empires
destroyers inherent in all
the history of humanity
of families and communities
of tribes and kings and states
the mutation of murder from misdeed
to policy
the talking, talking, talking,
in a multiplicity
of languages and literatures
and the continual definition of
new others
against whom we may define
ourselves
our “us,” their “them”
the depths of deep time and times
and times-after-time of the universe
or universes, or multiverses
and the comparative recency of life
and my birth
just three-quarters of a century ago
and waking up this morning
and now
in the whirl of all those billions of tiny waves
and unseen particles, wavicles and
unnameables,
some passing through my body, which,

I am told, is more space than matter
constantly interacting at blurring speeds
which a blurry mind can't fathom
let alone describe
and with the equally baffling billions of living things
(and almost living things) swarming
and, well, thriving throughout my own
self and body
in this origin of life, a soupy froth of twisted
genes
that replicate, and change, and
replicate, and change
and the permeable boundaries that leak, and
those through which we drink
allowing unnamed entities in and out
through my skin and open orifices
and the countless constancy
of all these vast activities,
along a seemingly well-protected border
but more akin to a crowded bazaar on market day
the capital economy that makes my bed, my
sheets, my house
the mathematics and motions that make the
thingness of my day
the braided tree that makes my lineage
and roots me to the past
and grows its leaves for when I'm gone
lines tangle, lies tell, names change
runaways and wanderers, heretics and heroes
the list to do today, and the unwritten things we have
forgotten or lost
the histories of ideas in all the books in all the world
the philosophical and mythic
and scientific or just odd

the growing and shrinking and evolving of canons
and singers and dancers and artists and actors
  makers of gestures, painters on walls
  storytellers, mythmakers, epic liars in all
  crafters of things, collectors of shells
  crazy beautiful people
    who decorate themselves
    with scars, tattoos, furs, or just clothes
  pot makers and stirrers and weavers of songs
  thieves, cheats, fibbers, and preachers
    those who fake and those who take
    those who hide and move on
    killers and devils who dwell in our trees
  the broken and lost
    the never to be found
  the families who keep hold of their own
  the bleeding, and dying,
    and suffering and sighing,
    and those who can take
    "Nothing by Mouth"
  our incapacity
    to reconcile
    all our tools of signification
    representations
    words
    names
      maps
      equations
      data points
    digital models
    simulacra
      sentences
      contracts
      songs

plays
poems
novels
symphonies
libraries and collections
creations lost to memory or museums,
buried or burned

And I say
there are not enough words for it, nor enough time
But remember, remember all you can
and wonder, and watch, and hope

On the Modern Denial of Null Messages

When I was a child
        television baby
Tuning and turning channels,
        I swallowed a decoder ring.

Mommy in the box
        always meant something
Even when I didn't understand.
        Watch, sit, wait, listen
        Check with the writers,
        On all my old detective shows
        nothing extraneous happened;
There were no miracles or accidents,
        no meaningless junk, no unfired guns.

So I learned to look
        for camera angles and cryptic meaning
And always imagined
        background music for myself.

The music would tell me
        Oh, it always does, like Captain Kirk
What is coming next, and
        whether it's good or bad.

Long time gone, academy years
        All the world was a stage,
But now it's a studio
        with everything calculated
For maximum effect, audience
        appeal, and purchasing power.

Heed the street electric
    croon now comfort alone
With blue tube mommy
    and earplug background band.
Keep working your decoder,
    You can script your own series.

One Theory of Salvation

Trundling back and forth
On homely paths
We wear a furrow
Work a chasm
Of what we have always known

The decorative striations
Of sedimentary strata
Are not unattractive
But useful facts
Insights or vision
May only be gleaned
Through obscure technology

Unprepared, equipped
Only with trowel and sieve
Or the requisite patience
To excavate our lives

We can be released
By the unexpected

The catastrophe
That tears down walls
Breaks the road before us
Carries away and down
Brings us to the edge
Precarious, yet balanced
We look out and away

Safety restored
Roads rebuilt

We still may move
Through tight
Closed channels
Or we may retain
The new horizon

Party with a Bad Band

Deaf, deaf
To have so long listened
To the din, din
Of the singerless song
But the beat, beat
Of the barbarous rhythm
Catches your body
Carries you, strong

So dance, dance
Sweet sweat runs and glistens
In the din, din
With the unmindful crowd
As the beat, beat
Of the musicless pounding
Loosens your body
Lets all be allowed
Until it ends, panting

The meaningless dancing
The fantasized freedom
Scatters about
With the rhythmless crowd
Done, down, back to the drinking
'Til more music sounds
Joyful and loud
Then hopeful but joyless
Return to the dancing,
Surrender your sorrow
To the grasp of the crowd

Pastoral Visit

shaded porch, wicker furniture
crickets
the lake rippling slowly
absolute dark and brilliant
stars

nights far from artificial light
          can disorient
but my city and I know one other

sirens are old acquaintances
singing and shouting supplant the squeaky
bugs
engines and voices buzz in counterpoint
like cyborg kazoos

a fish jumps
and I am surprised
the water lapping across the stones
is lovely at first
then monotonous and maddening
and keeps me awake
until I relax and allow it to fade
like long ago I learned with traffic and trains

to long absent eyes and ears
the once familiar becomes grotesque
the comfort comes
more in the leaving than in the visit

Perhaps Not a Poem

Perhaps I'm not a poet
I love the word
The feel of play and power
And yet I doubt
'Tis such a solemn role
To wrap around yourself
The mystery and sensitivity
The sublimity of passion
Might overwhelm me
Could I endure to stand
So strong encased in pride
As to make a monument of myself?

Life is hard enough
To understand, without
Making a secret of it,
Known only to the perfect souls
Of the chosen few

So I'll just play with words
No awesome names for me
I'll do my best to share
Confusion as well as
hopes, Fear along with
beauty, For those are what
I have

If I can take a fragment
Of my day, and have another
Live it over with me,
Then that is enough.
It need not be a poem.

The Reading Child

The reading child is asked:
Why don't you do something?
And is confused.

The reading child is told:
Put that book down and play outside.
And takes his book and hides, outside.

The reading child is called:
Four-eyes, grandpa, encyclopedia,
And takes his books home, and hides.

For the books and words are more powerful,
Better than all else around him,
        more rewarding,
More forgiving, and above all,
        they take him away
And he lives in words, and in words reveals
        himself,
And does not hide.

Reason

Reason has no motor
It starts not
Nor does it stop
But runs on
Indiscriminately

Permuting variables
Commuting sentences
Palpating prepositions

Reason has no mother
        no father and no lover
The origin of reasoning
        is not of reason itself
But
Of the same descent
        as dance
        and darting down the hill
        or laughing with friends

The joy is of the body
Not the words

Reconstruction

No, we are not finished.
Why does this offend you?
It is time now to rebuild.
We must scrape the surface of the earth.
We must mix it, heat it, beat it.
What is made over is made ours.
What has grown old must be made new.
We must replace it, bit by bit,
In nostalgia, like it was,
Or as it is remembered,
Or as we wish it to become,
Or as we believe
It should have been.
We have much to begin again,
And old tasks to begin anew.
Tear down the beams and bricks
To sort, transport, transform them,
To create and reconstruct.
Once the old has been demolished,
And the new no longer relished,
We shall revive
Our hopeful vision of the past.
No, we are not finished.
It shall never be complete.
Come, now, there is much to do.

Resurrection: The Silver Tree

As I recovered fragments
of old poems,
most were unremembered revelations,
a few,
very few,
were fond reminiscences,
but one,
clearly remembered,
which I sought repeatedly,
escaped me.

I wrote
"The Silver Tree"
in 1978,
in Baltimore,
in late summer,
in a small recessed park,
called The Dell,
on a warm early morning,
while my boys
did something or other
that I ignored
because I was
caught in a vision
as the morning light
illuminated
a stark skeletal tree
bright against its living siblings,
rooted at the top of an old wall,
elevated above the level
from which I viewed it,

floating, brilliant,
almost a silhouette,
but seemingly
in the trick of that morning light,
lit from within.

And so,
as I ignored my boys,
I wrote, entranced
by the pleasure
of my words,
coming smoothly,
quickly, sure
and effortless,
as I tried to capture
that sense
of the silver tree
dead but deathless,
shining,
bright in silent denial.

And I could not find that poem,
but I collected others,
and rejoiced in some,
discarded others,
rewrote many,
but kept looking.

Until I stopped.

But I went back
to mine that vein again
and LO!
There it was!

Not as I remembered it,
set out separately,
but appended,
tacked on,
to other observations
of those sultry days
when we went out early,
before the heat
and heavy air
drove us back inside.

So there it was:
recovered, fact.

And it was flat and colorless,
not the flash capture
of a momentary epiphany,
but a strained and cliched
struggle
to appear poetic.

All that remained
of any value
was a dim reminder
of how clearly
that sunlit corpse
stood out
silver
against the background
of the dark August green
survivors.

I tried to resurrect that poem;
it was beyond redemption

or resuscitation,
and yet
(I love that line,
and yet),
there was that memory,
that search and hope,
and that remnant
of ambition,
the will to write,
so,
there was something to preserve,
something,
to strive to bring back to life,
so instead,
there is this,
not
"The Silver Tree"
but
its memory and monument.

Return from a Northern Sojourn

I. First Spring Back

The light still surprises me.
I have learned two things:
What it is like here,
And what it was like there.
Those years have now become
Filled with cold and rain.
There were so few flowers.
In contrast, we have not found
What we thought we sought.
Instead,
We have been rewarded
By discovery.

II. Bus Stop Bench

In weary reverie
I watch my folded hands.
Bright light turns them white and creased.
Are they still?
Can they yet grip and seize?
Slowly, my eyes adjust
To see the steady pulsing
Of blood through clasped fingers.

I feel it then.
The wave and lap of
The sea of my self,
Lost for a while in waiting.
A roar in my ears

And I look up.
The forgotten street returns.
The bench hard,
Hands flutter.
Shadows and strengths are here.
The sun has moved on.
So have I.

III. Hometown

The crowded bus
Rises over a bridge.
We are suddenly released
From the narrow streets.

There is ample distance now
For horizon's haze to show itself,
For the gray and jagged skyline
To stretch its jumble in all directions.
City now, my city.

No hills loom above,
Just buildings and smoke.
Even traffic is a new-beloved thing.
There, the old tower, there.
Memories and past conspire,
Pulling us in,
In the city now, it is
Around, all around.
Old city, new home. Okay.

Reunion

They stood outside, the men in the family,
        oddly united.
Not milling, for a common consciousness
Told them milling was not appropriate,
        but they moved together.

Weight, height, bearing, build, color, clothes,
        All were assorted,
And all the living generations represented.
A few features repeated
Linking the lingering survivors:
        Nose and jowls,
        Jowls and ears,
        Ears and nose.

Death commanded the occasion,
But causes run far deeper.
And on the walk outside the funeral home
Those linked only by friendship or marriage,
        stretched and turned,
        stuffed hands in pockets,
Busied with a cigarette, on the fringe.
Bound by looser contracts,
        penned in ink,
        linked by time together,
        at work or at the bar,
        but not in blood.
The many bodied family
        gathered round this body of its blood.

Here, in the rituals of death,
        Deeper, older, more than flesh or blood

or bone,
Borne in the repetition of the minor themes,
Among these gathered members
Of the scattered family, the repetition of the minor themes,
        Nose, ears, jowls
        were hidden hints
Not in mourning but in tribute,
        even celebration of success,
That these genes, minuscule but active,
Had carried strong expeditions
                                into the ocean of humanity
And established colonies.

Some Poems, Broken in Five Lines

I

In summer heat
we move the fans
change rooms
to keep the air
moving as we wish

And still the wind
shifts direction,
rises, falls
the air stirs
and moves our fans

II

Public pain
is a rare sight in suburbia
In the development
it is easy to be ignorant
of your neighbor's suffering

Only the poor
display their lives in the open street
Without lawns or hedge
it is hard to achieve
the dignity of isolation

III

It had been so long
since I had shuffled
through high grass
on a summer morning,
I had forgotten the dew

Now my wet shoes
and the clinging blades
leave tracks behind
as I enter the library
of a great university

I am amused
that this should happen
near the main street
of this gritty city
so soon after leaving the country

IV

This perfect cheek
smooth as polished stone
curving to secret creases
printed on glossy paper
is impossible

The real, though round
is dusted in fine hairs
slick with sensual sweat
blooms to tender hand
and possesses blemishes

V

The clean pen
slices through thought
lays bare hopes
or on a passing glance
gives great joy

The right words
layer like onions
open eyes
the hidden heart
or a rich scent

Speak

There are so many words

And even more meanings

Significations spread out

like ants, wildflowers and stars

It is so difficult

To state the facts

How can we tell the truth?

Theory into Practice: Framed 9×10

For a while I submerged myself
In all the arcana of my craft
And yet ... I could not accomplish
Higher skill or new dexterity
But was left, introspect, immobile
It seems there's no greater crippler
Of creation than the canny hobble
Of a too subtle self-consciousness
The mirror is a morass, the pose
Too contrived, and the rest is nonsense

This Individual

. . . this individual,
What, do you suppose,
Would he be like?
        Other, of course, than free.
        Other than being
        Only his own man.
        Instead of being
        Independent and firm.

Is he loose inside?
Does he shake?
Do his bones rumble
        And grate, grinding
        As he enters the world?

Can he listen? Does he hear?
Could he stand to wait?
Will he stand bemused
By the beat of his own blood?

How does he see himself?
        A muscular or bony
        Frame of force?
        A bag of skin
        Full of juice and bowels?

How should we portray
His thinking, or his will?

Is he a distant watcher, amazed
At the storms and weathers of his
nerves?

Is he his own grim captain,
Hand on wheel, and eye to sky,
Voice bellowing to his engine room?

Is he the clean technician,
Clipboard, projects, and priorities,
Lists to check and carefully adjust?

This Individual,
From what is he divided?
Is he indivisible?

Waiting

The child at the window
Has its rubbery hands
Placed against the pane.
If only it were a puppet
What a masterwork
        of pathos
Nose pressed against the glass
Is small and flat and white
As only bloodless flesh can be
The eye rolls
Curiosity?
        Stuffed toy?
Resignation droops the lip

It is a terrible thing
For a child to become patient

Waking Dreams

1. Afternoon

The surface of the world
(the inner curving sweep of the globe of my vision)
Is crinkled like foil
Is seen through a brightly veined film
Is ribbed and pulsing as a living crystal cell

The oil of this limned scene
        (thick grainy medium
        of the surface of the cerebrum)
Has been ignited by my hot eyes
Has been scarred and broken by a wire whip
Has been cracked by time and dimmed by rank and evil air

The frame of this mad film
        (flickering light
        of protracted and projected fevers)
Focused where I never look
Will not turn to let me see myself
Is cut and spliced by machetes and wax

2. Before Dawn

When you awake in fear
        a jerk
        a drop
        back into bed
        quick breath
        beating heart
Remember this:

It has always been so

The hunting cat
Came with click of claws on stone
Over embers of a fire
That accidentally died

The blond raiders
Came up from the boats
With axes and arrows
And a cheerful yell

The dread spirits
Heeded not offerings nor curse
And spread from house to house
Bringing fever and sure death

The sharp knocking
Brought you to your door
And to the hard men
Who took you away

The high machines
Carried a constant threat
And you had no control
Over when it came

When your fear subsides
And you've told yourself
That it was nothing
And gone back to sleep,
Remember, waking
    You have lied

Walking Railroad Track Revelation

I.

Going to work
Reluctantly
Keeping on
Nearly late
Pushing fast
Hot sidewalk
Muscles straining
Bumpy rhythm
Breathing hard
Smoky lungs
Sore feet sliding
In vain boots
Throat tightening
Hating the evening shift
Red lights flashing at the crosswalk

Well hell, if the train's going to come
Might as well take your time
Sure, you're late, but it's not for not
trying

So — you slow and look
down the long line of cars
And settle against a post
to wait while they go by

II.

There is a potent medicine
A trap for eyes and minds

In the spinning clicking wheels of the railroad

The optical illusions of
        The headlights of the cars

Through the spinning clicking wheels of the
        railroad

Draw you in your fascination
        Toward a hypnotized release

By the spinning clicking wheels of the railroad

But a remnant of revulsion
        Fights the siren in the song

Of the spinning clicking wheels of the railroad

And that impulse for survival
        Keeps your body safe from harm

From the spinning clicking wheels of the
        railroad

III.

Whoo! What a long train of coal and cars
Pull away from the wheels
That tempt in their offer of mutilation
And welcome the caboose
That promises release
In the rattle of the rail as the end comes near

Stretch up and forward, away from the post
Ready to cross the track bed's ridge
Wave to the conductor,
        train gone, baby, gone
        rush and rumble and rattle away
Start walking again,
        carrying your hurry like a cross

The gentle rise of the track bank slows you
Tugging hard on the muscles of your legs
Look both ways, old stories remind you
        of the second train
        unheard, seen too late

The fear never quite casts out
        the attraction
        and revulsion

IV.

Climbing to the top of the track,
Summit of a minor man-made mound
Looking up, eyes and mind together,
Surprised by a momentary vision

The hills are green going brown,
But graying in the dusk
They never hurry, not to work, not to a railroad death

The sky is evening indigo,
Graying into black,
And domes over rail and river and asphalt

Buildings and people shimmer

In the memory of other days
Floods, bright sun, rain and mud,
Morning fog, leaves and flurries

There are clear moments
        When the movements and the edges
All spin in the kaleidoscope of understanding
        Brighter than the bits of glass,
Then all join together
        As their sudden silent pattern
Stuns you, then falls away

Water in a Sieve

hold your breath
wait no
hold your mind
breathe slow

and
smooth
take no notice of it

now
search your mind
that idea

was slippery
can you grasp it?
open your eyes
but do not look
fix your vision at the edges
then move slowly
back to center
in the void
take your mind
beyond your head
let it fill your whole body
ride the tide of your blood
breathe
and breathe again
feel the quick deep relief
at the bottom of
your lungs
good
you are still alive

What Will Become of Me?

If I write poetry,
        Will I be left-handed?

If I catch my dreams,
        And keep them as boxed treasures
        Of both night and day,
Will new dreams fear me?

If I climb the red tree
        Growing within me, will I
        Fall and fall, down and back
Through the long lines of our blood?

If I seize the woman
        And enter, as she enters me,
        Will we ever be one?
Or never two again?

If I let me live,
        Who then, will let me be?

When Crows Follow Me

If I be by this sign blessed
Am I an uninvited guest?
The residents of this sweet park
View me with such calm regret
My cawed accompaniment is stark
My followers request respect
Can special favors come unmixed?
Are sidelong glances now resentful?
Recognition has odd tricks
Uneasiness is not respectful
If mystic stigmata are a test
The mockingbird would suit me best

Winding Up: Spiral Notebook Conclusion

(or back to the beginning)

As I write
The last poem in this book
(a spiral pad, for stenography)
I find I've reached the front

These days and hours
I have tried to write
Been eager
And clamped and closed

Yet I never knew
Somehow, way back then,
When this was all but new
I started backwards

I think that in my search
        turning stones
        digging holes
        reading clouds
        deciphering ripples of water
That I shall find this
        insignificant

Acknowledgments

Poetry has been part of my life since childhood. My mother read poetry to us aloud and introduced me to her favorites, Henry Wadsworth Longfellow, Vachel Lindsay, Carl Sandburg, Dorothy Parker, and Don Marquis. I also grew up with a wonderful ten-volume anthology, edited by Charles H. Sylvester and first published in 1901, titled *Journeys Through Bookland.*

I thank Dorothy Martin, my English teacher and adviser for the high school paper, for the early guidance and encouragement that I received in writing poetry. What little craft and discipline I have learned was in her classes. I have had no formal training or classes since, although I have enjoyed some writers' conferences and retreats.

Thanks also to Tom Hoyer, who read many of these poems more than twenty years ago and offered lasting comments; to Caroline Banks, who read them more recently and gave great counsel and encouragement; and to my former publisher and editor, Leigh E. Rich, who reviewed many of them.

The Author

For more than fifty years, Marc Thomas has written occasional fragments that he calls poetry. His wife Margo has regularly prodded him to publish them. He finally listened to her.

Marc has been a college librarian, a historical society archivist, and a government technocrat. In 2006, he retired from the Centers for Medicare and Medicaid Services.

He has a bachelor's degree from The Johns Hopkins University and masters degrees in library and information science from the State University of New York at Albany and in theology from the Ecumenical Institute of St. Mary's Seminary and University in Baltimore.

Marc is active in several book clubs, he is an avid and eclectic reader. He also supports Little Free Libraries, including the one in front of his house.

In 2011, Marc and his wife retired to Savannah, Georgia.

Since the COVID pandemic, which resulted in the compilation of the first edition of this book, he has become an active and amused poet, and frequently reads his poems at Savannah open mics.

He has published several other books of poetry. His work can be found on his website:

The Ruminating Poet Press,
www.ruminatingpoetpress.com.

www.ingramcontent.com/pod-product-compliance
Lightning Source LLC
LaVergne TN
LVHW090615110826
845146LV00001B/395

* 9 7 9 8 9 9 2 5 8 1 1 4 0 *